BEASTLY BIOMES

CARLY ALLEN-FLETCHER

Creston Books

Wherever you go on our planet, you will find animals living in many different types of places.

Scientists call these places BIOMES. Each biome has its own special properties.

Our planet can be divided into many small biomes, but there are five main types.

AQUATIC: Any place with water. These are salty — oceans, seas, coral reefs, and estuaries (where rivers join seas) — and fresh water — rivers, lakes, ponds, and wetlands.

FOREST: Tropical and temperate rainforests. These can be cold taiga forests in the north (also called boreal forests, full of evergreen trees that never lose their leaves) or deciduous forests where the leaves on the trees change color and fall off every year.

GRASSLAND: Large flat areas and hills covered with grass and flowers. Plains, savannas, and steppes are all grasslands and are often home to vast herds of roaming animals.

DESERT: Dry regions with little rainfall. Usually, deserts are sandy and rocky, but anywhere with scarce rain counts as a desert biome. Antarctica has giant deserts, even though it's not hot or sandy.

TUNDRA: Cold rocky places where there are strong winds and no trees. Only lichen and small shrubs can survive here. The Arctic tundra is found near the North and South poles. Alpine tundra is found all over the world on the tops of high mountains.

Let's take a closer look and see what animals live in each biome.

The biggest part of the aquatic biome is the MARINE one, which makes up most of our planet. Deep oceans and salty seas cover over 70% of the world's surface.

BLUE WHALES swim all over the world.

GIANT SQUID and CURLED OCTOPUSES drift around the cold waters of the North Atlantic Ocean.

SHIHO'S SEAHORSES dart through the colorful coral reefs of the Sea of Japan.

WANDERING ALBATROSSES
soar over the oceans around
the South Pole.

ATLANTIC BLUEFIN TUNA swim in big schools
all over the Atlantic Ocean.

ROYAL STARFISH
lie on seashores
around the
Pacific Coast.

WOBBEGONGS are a kind of shark
that blend in with the stony sea
bottom around the coast of Australia.

FRESHWATER rivers and lakes are part of the aquatic biome, too. From tiny streams to rushing rivers and lakes, they are full of life.

HIPPOS submerge themselves in the waters of East Africa.

MANDARIN DUCKS glide in the lakes of East Asia and Europe.

BLACK POND TURTLES swim in the ponds and rivers of Bangladesh and India.

DAMSELFLIES hover above ponds throughout the world, catching tiny insects to eat.

AXOLOTLS paddle around the bottom of Mexican lakes.

WATER VOLES splash in streams all over Europe and Russia.

REEDFISHES wiggle through the reeds of African rivers.

YAPOKS dive in the rivers of Central America. Also called the water opossum, this is the only aquatic marsupial.

XINGU RAY FISHES glide along the bottom of the Xingu river in Brazil.

The WETLANDS are also part of the Aquatic biome. Wetlands are places where land meets water, like swamps, salt marshes, and bogs. They also include estuaries, where rivers meet the sea. These places are favorites for all kinds of animals.

INDIAN BOARS wallow in the swamps of India and Nepal.

BLUE CRABS scuttle around estuaries along the east coast of the Americas.

Bright red TOMATO FROGS hop around the swamps of Madagascar.

SALTWATER CROCODILES lurk in estuaries and swamps in Australia and Asia.

SNOWY EGRETS forage for food in the muddy estuaries of the Americas.

EMPEROR DRAGONFLIES dart from reed to reed in the marshes of Europe while JACK SNIPES wade nearby.

RAINFORESTS belong to the forest biome. They are warm and wet, getting lots of rain. Temperate rainforests are cooler than tropical rainforests and mostly found by the coast. Thousands of different species live in tropical and temperate rainforests.

ELEGANT SUNBIRDS perch deep in the forests of Sangihe Island, Indonesia.

DE BRAZZA'S MONKEYS scamper up trees in central Africa.

CASSOWARIES peck at fruit in the rainforests of Australia and New Guinea, while ULYSSES BUTTERFLIES flit though the trees.

BANANA SLUGS slither over the floor of North America's giant redwood forests.

BENGAL SLOW LORISES clamber through the rainforests of India and China.

EMERALD TREE BOAS glide through the branches of the Amazon Rainforest.

PACIFIC SALMON spawn in the creeks of coastal temperate rainforests in North America before swimming upstream.

VENCES' CHAMELEONS blend into the leaves deep in the jungles of Madagascar.

DECIDUOUS FORESTS are found in cooler, rainy areas. In deciduous forests and woodlands, the leaves change color and fall off in autumn. These forests provide a home for many kinds of animals.

RED FOXES dig their burrows all over the Northern Hemisphere.

JEWEL BEETLES scurry around forests all over the world.

APENNINE YELLOW-BELLIED TOADS splash in forest pools in Italy.

HEDGEHOGS curl up in Europe, Asia, and Africa.

RACCOONS search for food in the forests of North America.

OVENBIRDS build their nests in the Eastern United States.

IRIOMOTE CATS prowl the forests of Iriomote Island, Japan.

TAIGA FORESTS, also called boreal or snow forests, are the earth's largest land biome. Growing only in the northern hemisphere, they feature coniferous trees like pine, fir, and spruce.

SIBERIAN TIGERS roam the northern forests of Russia.

BOBCATS and SNOWSHOE HARES leave tracks all over North America.

SIBERIAN SALAMANDERS survive the cold winters by freezing themselves in ice during hibernation, then thawing out in spring.

RED CROSSBILLS peck at pine nuts in forests all over Northern Europe.

REINDEER graze in the far north of Europe and Russia.

GREY WOLVES hunt in the snowy forests of Northern Europe.

KODIAK BEARS fish for salmon in Alaska and Canada.

The ALPINE TUNDRA lies high up on mountains. Because of the altitude, it is too windy and cold for trees to grow, but hardy grasses and shrubs cling to the slopes. Unlike the other biomes, alpine tundra often form smaller areas.

LLAMAS climb the Andes of South America.

ALPINE ARGUS BUTTERFLIES flutter through the snowy Alps of Europe.

HIMALAYAN TAHRS graze in the steep mountains of northern India.

KEA PARROTS nest in the cold heights of New Zealand.

YAKS lick moss off rocks in Tibet and the Himalayas.

PIKAS nibble grass on the mountainsides of Asia.

VIVIPAROUS LIZARDS burrow in the mountains of Northern Europe and Central Asia.

The ARCTIC TUNDRA is near the North and South Poles. Most Arctic tundra is around the North Pole, while the South Pole only has a few small tundra areas. Trees cannot grow in the frozen and rocky ground. Lichen, moss, and small shrubs are the only plants that can survive.

MUSK OXEN graze on moss and lichen around the Arctic circle.

ARCTIC FOXES curl up in the snows of northern Europe.

LEMMINGS dig tunnels to stay warm under the snow on the North Pole.

SOUTH POLAR SKUAS nest on the rocky shores of Antarctica before flying north for the winter.

ATLANTIC PUFFINS crowd cliffsides all over the Arctic circle to breed.

ARCTIC WOOLLY BEAR CATERPILLARS freeze solid over the winter, then thaw out in the summer and transform into moths in the Arctic circle.

ARCTIC BUMBLEBEES buzz through the sparse shrubs of the North Pole.

A desert is defined by the amount of rainfall it gets. Any place that gets less than ten inches of rain a year counts as a desert. The biggest deserts in the world are in Antarctica (the South Pole) and the Arctic (the North Pole). These are called POLAR DESERTS.

ADELIE PENGUINS huddle together in Antarctica.

LEOPARD SEALS splash in the waters of Antarctica.

POLAR BEARS travel long distances over the northern ice in search of food.

ARCTIC TERNS fly from Antarctica to the Arctic every year.

WALRUSES laze around on the ice floes of the Arctic.

PTARMIGANS race over the snows of the Arctic.

COLD DESERTS are often found in high places near mountains. Sometimes they are called semi-arid deserts. Warmer than polar deserts, but much colder than hot deserts, they have very cold winters and very hot summers.

GOLDEN EAGLES and CALIFORNIA CONDORS soar over deserts in North America.

BACTRIAN CAMELS trek across the deserts of China.

BIGHORN SHEEP clamber along the craggy rocks in North American deserts.

SNOW LEOPARDS prowl and GOBI BEARS scavenge for food in the Gobi desert of Asia.

PATAGONIAN FOXES trot through the deserts of South America.

DID YOU KNOW?

Squirrels four front teeth grow about 6 inches every year.

SQUIRREL APPRECIATION DAY
JANUARY 21

HOT DESERTS have scorching hot summers and milder winters. These are the deserts we usually imagine, with sandy dunes and large areas of hard rocky ground. Plants here are tough, like cacti, tumbleweeds, and desert wildflowers. Also called sub-tropical deserts, they are found in Africa, South America, Asia, and Australia.

GILA MONSTERS bask on the warm rocks of South American deserts.

DIADEM SNAKES sun-bathe by the entrance to their nests in North African deserts.

QUOLLS hide in their dens in the Australian Outback, while NUMBATS catch termites with their long tongues.

DESERT LIONS roar in the deserts of Namibia, searching for OSTRICHES to hunt.

DESERT TAWNY OWLS peer around for GRASSHOPPERS to catch in the deserts of Israel and Saudi Arabia.

SAVANNAS are a type of grassland biome that are often found around the edges of hot deserts. They have vast areas of grass with an occasional clump of trees and are most common in South America, Africa, and Asia. In South Africa, these grassy places are also known as the veld.

HOOPOE BIRDS peck the ground for worms and bugs in savannas all over the world.

INDIAN PANGOLINS lap up ants and termites across India and South Asia.

GIRAFFES eat the leaves of acacia trees in Africa.

BONGO ANTELOPES and AFRICAN ELEPHANTS gather at watering holes in the African savanna.

MENELAUS BLUE MORPHO BUTTERFLIES flutter all over the Cerrado, a vast grassland in Brazil.

AFRICAN BULLFROGS bury themselves in the African mud when it gets too hot.

PLAINS are the other main type of grassland biome. They cover large expanses and are found on many continents. Cooler than savannas, they feature rolling hills with grass, flowers, and herbs but no trees. They are known as prairies, steppes, uplands, and pampas in different parts of the world.

PALLAS'S CATS live in rocky crevices and caves on the steppes of Mongolia, while TAKHIS gallop nearby.

MARBLED POLECATS hunt on the steppes of China.

HORSFIELD'S TORTOISES dig burrows in the Russian plains.

HONEY BUZZARDS hunt in the uplands of Europe and fly to Africa for the winter.

Herds of BISON graze the prairies of North America.

GIANT ARMADILLOS wander the pampas of South America.

TAKAHES scurry through the high grasslands in New Zealand.

2% FRESHWATER
3% GRASSLAND
7% TUNDRA
9.5% DESERT
9.5% FOREST
69 % MARINE

The biomes of our world are beautiful and
vast, full of creatures big and small.

All over the Earth, in every kind of biome,
animals find a way to make a home.

What is your biome?

Where is your home?

What animals do you share it with?